Becoming a SUPREME COURT JUSTICE

By Barbara M. Linde

Gareth Stevens
PUBLISHING

Please visit our website, www.garethstevens.com. For a free color catalog of all our high-quality books, call toll free 1-800-542-2595 or fax 1-877-542-2596.

Thank you to the following teachers for their insights: Patricia Garland, Pennridge School District, Perkasie, PA; Gail Housman, Ideal Elementary School, Countryside, IL.

Library of Congress Cataloging-in-Publication Data

Linde, Barbara M., author.
 Becoming a Supreme Court justice / Barbara M. Linde.
     pages cm. — (Who's your candidate? choosing government leaders)
 Includes index.
 ISBN 978-1-4824-4051-5 (pbk.)
 ISBN 978-1-4824-4052-2 (6 pack)
 ISBN 978-1-4824-4053-9 (library binding)
 1. United States. Supreme Court—Juvenile literature. 2. Judges—United States—Juvenile literature. 3. United States—Politics and government—Juvenile literature. I. Title.
 KF8742.L55 2015
 347.73'2634—dc23
                                        2015028862

Published in 2016 by
Gareth Stevens Publishing
111 East 14th Street, Suite 349
New York, NY 10003

Copyright © 2016 Gareth Stevens Publishing

Designer: Andrea Davison-Bartolotta
Editor: Kristen Nelson

Photo credits: Cover, p. 1 (girl) Brand New Images/Getty Images; cover, p. 1 (background) Chuck Kennedy/MCT/ Getty Images; p. 4 Roger L. Wollenberg/Pool via Bloomberg/Getty Images; p. 5 jiawangkun/Shutterstock.com; p. 6 courtesy of the Library of Congress; p. 7 (White House, Capitol) Vector pro/Shutterstock.com; p. 7 (Supreme Court Building) The Winner/Shutterstock.com; p. 8 De Visu/Shutterstock.com; p. 9 KidStock/Getty Images; p. 11 David Hume Kennerly/Getty Images; pp. 12–13 Pablo Martinez Monsivias-Pool/Getty Images; p. 15 SW Productions/Getty Images; pp. 16–17 Caiaimage/Tom Merton/Getty Images; p. 19 Nicholas Prior/Getty Images; p. 20 Paul J. Richards/AFP/Getty Images; p. 21 Cynthia Johnson/Getty Images; p. 23 Buyenlarge/Getty Images; p. 24 Larry Downing-Pool/Getty Images; p. 25 (inset) flySnow/iStock/Thinkstock; p. 25 (main) davidevison/iStock/ Thinkstock; p. 27 Carl Iwasaki/The LIFE Images Collection/Getty Images; p. 28 Rob Marmion/Shutterstock.com; p. 29 graphixmania/Shutterstock.com.

Printed in the United States of America

CPSIA compliance information: Batch #CW16GS: For further information contact Gareth Stevens, New York, New York at 1-800-542-2595.

CONTENTS

Words in the glossary appear in **bold** type the first time they are used in the text.

Suppose some students are throwing food in the lunchroom and are sent to the principal. Without hearing their side of the story, all the students are punished. One student says he was there, but wasn't part of the problem. His class **representative** takes the case to the school **disciplinary** board.

You're a student member of the board. You listen to both sides—the student and the cafeteria worker. You carefully read the school rules with your fellow board members. Then you help make a decision.

Being part of a school disciplinary group is somewhat like serving as a member of the United States Supreme Court! It can prepare you for a future in the court.

Supreme Court Justices, 2010

In the court

A Supreme Court justice is a member of the **judicial** branch of the US government. Congress first set the number of justices at six in 1789. That number has changed over the years, and today there are nine justices. They're called justices, not judges, to show that they're different from members of the lower courts, or the other courts in the country.

Like the Supreme Court justices, your work on a disciplinary board or student court could affect many students at your school. The decision could set a precedent, or example, for future cases and outcomes.

Checks and Balances

The US government is made up of three branches. Each branch makes sure that the other two branches don't have too much power. In this way, the rights of citizens stay at the center of the government. This arrangement is called checks and balances.

The legislative branch, made up of the House of Representatives and the Senate, makes the laws. The executive branch carries out the laws. The president, the vice president, the president's cabinet, and federal agencies make up the executive branch. The judicial branch says if the laws are legal according to the US **Constitution**. The Supreme Court and lower courts make up the judicial branch.

Your Turn!

The presence of students on a school court or disciplinary committee is a lot like the checks and balances of the US government. Students like you offer teachers and other adults a point of view they might not otherwise consider. It's a big responsibility.

US Constitution

3 Branches of Government

Legislative
(makes laws)

■ Congress

├ **Senate**

100 elected senators total

2 senators per state

└ **House of Representatives**

435 elected representatives total

representatives based on each state's population

Executive
(carries out laws)

■ President

├ **Vice President**

└ **Cabinet**

group of advisors chosen by the president and approved by the Senate

Judicial
(evaluates laws)

■ Supreme Court

nine justices sit at a time; presidents appoint and the Senate approves

■ Other Federal Courts

Each branch of the government has its own work to do, but all branches work together to make sure the country runs smoothly.

Who Qualifies?

The Constitution established the Supreme Court with justices appointed by the president. It was up to Congress to form lower courts around it, which it did in the Judiciary Act of 1789.

Although the Constitution doesn't say what a justice's qualifications should be, all have been lawyers or studied law. Many justices worked as lawyers in lower courts for years and even argued cases before the Supreme Court. Some have been judges in lower courts. All must have a good record of public service. Their professional lives must be top notch, and they should be honest and upstanding citizens in their personal lives.

Your Turn!

Your school might have qualifications for those running for student leadership positions. Be sure your grades are as good as they can be in all subject areas. Take part in school and community service projects. Work on being calm, honest, fair, and a good listener.

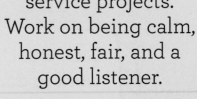

Sometimes students are asked to be part of a school court. Teachers may nominate, or suggest, you for the position because of your quality classwork, good attitude, and respect for others.

The Nomination Process

As long as a justice does the job properly, he or she keeps the office for life. However, there are only nine justices, so openings don't come around too often.

When the court needs a new justice, the president nominates someone. The president commonly has a list of people in mind. Most of the time, the president knows them. The president often wants someone of the same political party, especially someone who has similar ideas about how the country and government should be run. The president narrows down the choices and then announces the name of the nominee.

Lasting Influence

In 1981, President Reagan's nominee, Sandra Day O'Connor, became the first woman on the Supreme Court. Her appointment encouraged many women to go to law school and to enter politics. Many people credit her with helping women get better rights under the law. O'Connor retired from the Supreme Court in 2006.

Becoming a Supreme Court justice may take weeks or months. Justice O'Connor was nominated on August 19, 1981, and approved for the position on September 21, 1981.

A group in the Senate called the Judiciary Committee collects information, or knowledge, about the nominee. The senators want to find out as much as they can about the person's beliefs and past actions to make sure the person is qualified for the job of Supreme Court justice.

Your Turn!

Think about the reasons you might want to be part of a school court or disciplinary committee. Make a list of reasons that includes examples of how you've shown fairness, patience, and responsibility in the past. Have you helped another student in class or helped others to understand rules? Were you an important part of the **debate** team's wins this year?

FEINGOLD   MRS. FEINSTEIN

The Senate holds hearings where they ask the nominee many challenging questions. These hearings can be very long and tiring. After the hearings are finished, the entire Senate votes on the nominee. Most nominees are accepted. When a nominee isn't approved, the president starts the process over with another nominee.

In 2010, Elena Kagan was nominated by President Barack Obama to be a Supreme Court justice. Her nomination was confirmed 63-37 after many hours of hearings.

Your Campaign!

Like the Supreme Court, some student judges are nominated, either by one person or a group. If you want to be nominated, it's a good idea to let the right people know! You might talk directly to someone, or you might have a good friend talk for you.

If the judges are elected, then you need to build your campaign. You'll need some friends to help you. You may want to make flyers or posters. Perhaps you'll set up a website or appear on your school's TV station. You can attend school fairs, dances, and club meetings. Get your name out there as often as you can!

Political Parties

Justices commonly have connections to a political party, the groups that work to get things done in government. However, when they are making decisions, they're supposed to be **impartial**. This way, all citizens are treated fairly. However, keeping personal and party ideas out of decisions isn't easy. Many Supreme Court decisions are divided on party lines.

Whether you're trying to get elected or nominated, you'll need a platform, or a main message, for your campaign. Remember the reason you want to be a student judge or other leader to begin with! Do you want to help end bullying? Do you think rules about students' actions are enforced fairly? Your platform should be something that matters to you.

Talking with teachers and other adults is an important step in deciding your platform. They can help you decide whether any goal you have is doable. Talking to an older student who has been in the position you want would help you, too.

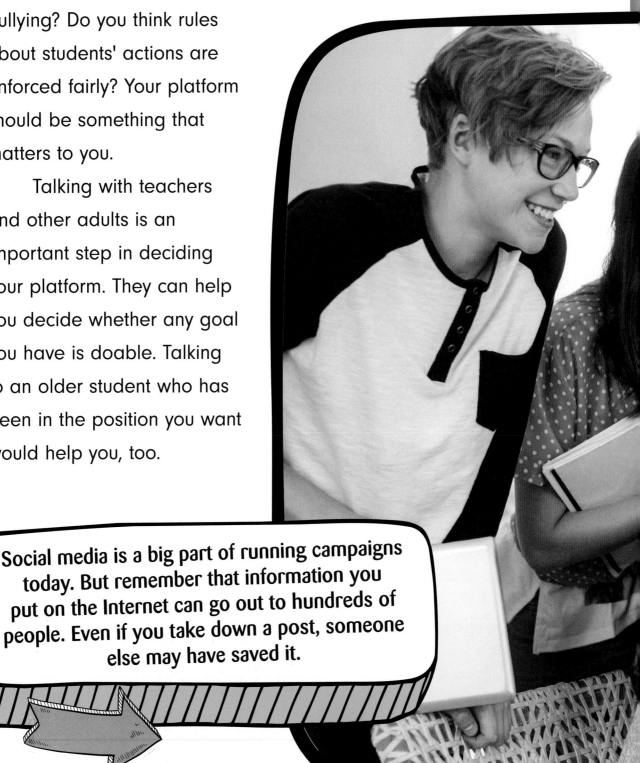

Social media is a big part of running campaigns today. But remember that information you put on the Internet can go out to hundreds of people. Even if you take down a post, someone else may have saved it.

If you're thinking of running for office, be careful what you say and what pictures you post on social media. It's pretty easy for anyone to find something you said or did and bring it up during your campaign. You don't want to lose because of a silly mistake.

How Would You Answer?

The following questions are modeled on the questions that US Supreme Court nominees might have to answer. Some are about hard situations you may face serving on a student court!

- Why do you want this job?

- Do you think your personal opinions and experience should influence your decisions?

- How closely would you follow the school rules when making a decision?

- Should the school officials have the right to say what a student can post on a school website?

- Does a dress code take away students' rights?

- Should students be punished if they pretend that something, like a ruler or a pencil, is a gun?

Your Turn!

Supreme Court justices need a deep understanding of the Constitution. If you want to be a student judge, you'll need to know your school handbook and rules inside out! The school probably has records of decisions other judges made. Read these carefully and think about how you might rule on the topics.

Public speaking is a big part of being a Supreme Court justice and would likely be part of working on a student court. Practice answering questions like these to your family and friends to get better at speaking to a group!

19

The Oath of Office

Once a justice has been approved, he or she takes two **oaths** of office. The chief justice administers, or gives, the oaths to the new justice.

In the Constitutional Oath, the justice says, "I, _____, do solemnly swear that I will support and defend the Constitution of the United States against all enemies." In the Judicial Oath, the justice promises to "administer justice without respect to persons, and do equal right to the poor and to the rich."

The ceremony may be public or private, or split between the two. Sometimes family and friends attend. The president might be there, too!

Supreme Court Traditions

Just before taking the oaths, the new justice sits in the chair that belonged to the first chief justice, John Marshall. After taking the oaths, the new justice and the chief justice walk down the steps of the Supreme Court building, both wearing their black robe.

The chief justice is the head justice on the Supreme Court. Warren Burger was chief justice from 1969 to 1986.

Getting Down to Work

The justices decide which cases they hear. They get thousands of requests each year, but they only hear **oral** arguments for about 80 cases. They make decisions on about 50 more cases, but don't hear arguments on these.

Each session of the Supreme Court's oral-argument days begins the same way. Shortly before it's time for the argument, a buzzer goes off in each justice's chamber, or room. They all go to the robing room and put on a plain black robe. Each justice shakes hands with every other justice. This shows that they may have different opinions, but they all have the same purpose.

What to Hear?

The Supreme Court doesn't hear just any court case! They only consider cases that may challenge a federal law or part of the Constitution. Most often, these cases are **appeals** from lower courts. Four justices must vote "yes" for the case to come before the Supreme Court.

The Supreme Court justices are some of the sharpest legal minds in the country.

Then the justices line up in order of **seniority** and walk into the courtroom. The chief justice sits in the middle. The next two most senior justices sit next to the chief justice on each side.

Each side gets 30 minutes to present their case. The justices listen carefully and ask questions. After the hearing, the justices discuss the case in secret. Then they make a decision, which is written out in the majority opinion. That doesn't mean all the justices agree! Those in the minority may write a minority opinion to explain their reasons for voting against a decision.

Chief Justice John Roberts

Your Turn!

The justices write their opinions to give reasons for every decision. How's your opinion or argument writing? Practice writing out your opinion about a school or family rule. Write one opinion that agrees with the rule and one that disagrees. Make sure your writing is clear and makes sense.

The Supreme Court has the final word about a case. No other court or lawmaker in the whole country can change a Supreme Court decision.

Historic Supreme Court Decisions

Some Supreme Court decisions change millions of lives! Here are just a few.

Brown v. Board of Education, 1954. African American children, like Linda Brown, often walked miles, passing all-white schools, to get to their all-black schools. The court said that **segregation** in public schools was against the Constitution. This overturned an older Supreme Court ruling on the subject in the 1896 case *Plessy v. Ferguson.*

New York Times v. Sullivan, 1964. A police chief sued the *New York Times* and four ministers for an ad in the newspaper. The ad said the chief arrested Martin Luther King Jr. to stop **integration**. The court said the newspaper and the ministers were covered by the First Amendment's protection of freedom of the press and freedom of speech.

Miranda v. Arizona, 1966. Ernesto Miranda wasn't told he could talk to a lawyer or remain silent when he was arrested. He was found guilty of a crime. The court said that the police always have to tell those accused of crimes their constitutional rights.

Your Turn!

How do you think you would rule in these cases as a Supreme Court justice? You might not get problems as difficult as these at school, but your decisions will matter. You may be able to change unjust rules and make life better for other students.

Linda Brown was 9 years old when she was allowed to start school at Sumner Elementary in Topeka, Kansas, after the *Brown v. Board of Education* case ended school segregation.

You—A Supreme Court Justice!

There are things you can do now to prepare for a career as a justice. Take part in school and community committees that make decisions. Join the debate team or a student political group.

Learn all you can about the Constitution. Talk to local judges and lawyers, and visit courtrooms. The Supreme Court publishes all its decisions. Have an adult read some of them with you. Talk about them so you understand them.

Today, justices are some of the most educated people in the country! Keeping up with your schoolwork and maintaining good grades are very important to your future on the court!

Young and Old

Joseph Story was just 32 when he joined the court in 1811. He had no experience as a judge, but he studied law and was a member of the Massachusetts House of Representatives. Oliver Wendell Holmes remained a Supreme Court justice until he was 90 years old!

Join the Supreme Court.
Here it is, your dream come true—with lots of hard work!

Become a judge for a lower court.
Many Supreme Court justices start out in lower courts.

Work for a law firm.
Become the best lawyer you can be.

Clerk.
Work for a local judge or even a Supreme Court justice!

Go to law school.
All the current justices went to either Harvard, Yale, or Columbia!

Go to college.
Learn all you can about history and politics. Make sure you have excellent reading and writing skills.

Join student government.
Take as many jobs in student government as you can, all the way through school.

GLOSSARY

appeal: a legal process by which a case decided in a lower court is brought to a higher court to review the decision

constitution: the basic laws by which a country or state is governed

debate: having to do with formal public discussion or argument

disciplinary: having to do with punishment

impartial: fair; treating all people the same

integration: the act of opening a group, community, or place to all people

judicial: having to do with justice and the courts

oath: a formal promise

oral: spoken

representative: one who stands for a group of people

segregation: the forced separation of races or classes

seniority: the status gained by the length of time of continuous service in a position

FOR MORE INFORMATION

BOOKS

Benoit, Peter. *The Supreme Court.* New York, NY: Children's Press, 2014.

Jakubiak, David J. *What Does a Supreme Court Justice Do?* New York, NY: PowerKids Press, 2010.

Krull, Kathleen. *Sonia Sotomayor.* New York, NY: Bloomsbury, 2015.

WEBSITES

About the Supreme Court
www.supremecourt.gov/about/about.aspx
Learn about the history of the Supreme Court, and get information about its important decisions.

The Supreme Court Justices
www.congressforkids.net/Judicialbranch_justices.htm
Find out how the judicial branch of our government works.